GRAPHICLEARNING INTEGRATED SOCIAL STUDIES

AT HOME

AND AT SCHOOL

HERE AND FAR AWAY
NOW AND LONG AGO

GRAPHICLEARNING
A Division of ABRAMS & COMPANY Publishers, Inc.
Waterbury, Connecticut

STUDENT
RESOURCE
BOOK

We Are Alike and Different

 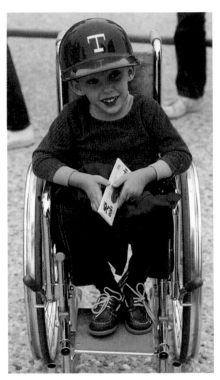 

Getting to School Safely

The Four Seasons

A We clean up.

B We never touch wild animals.

C We feed the birds.

D We plant a tree.

Seasons Across the United States

A

B

C

D

Seasons are not the same everywhere.

Citizenship at School

A

B

C

D

We are good citizens.

Safety at School

A We play safely.

B We learn about fire safety.

11

Schools Have Rooms

Everybody needs space.

A Map View

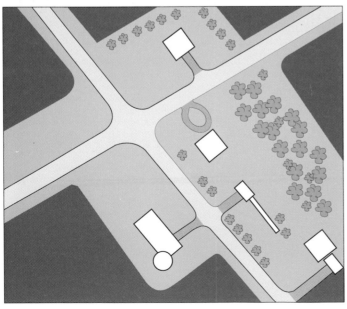

Map Key

☐	House
▭	Garage
▭	Shed
○▭	Barn and Silo
▬▬	Road
🌳🌲	Trees

Schools Long Ago

Children went to school long ago.

Schools Far Away

In some ways, France is like the United States.
In some ways, it is different.

In some ways, school in France is
like school in the United States.
In some ways, it is different.

Getting to School Long Ago

A

B

C

D

We get to school in different ways.
Children long ago got to school in
different ways, too.

Getting to School in a Faraway Place

A

B

Children in India go to school.

FAMILIES

My Family Long Ago

Otto   Bertha
Elsa's Parents
1924

Helen   Bernard
Paul's Parents
1922

Stanislaus   Sophie
Dorothy's Parents
1915

Maureen Timothy
Frank's Parents
1917

Elsa   Paul
Sam's Mother Sam's Father
1952

Dorothy   Frank
Mary's Mother   Mary's Father
1953

Sam   Mary
Lisa's Father   Lisa's Mother
1992

Lisa
1992

Family Roles

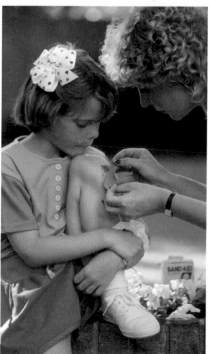

Our parents care for us.

Helping Each Other in a Family

A

B

C

D

Family members have needs.

Working Together in a Family

A

B

C

D

E

F

We try to be good family members.

Families Far Away

In some ways, families in Japan are
like families in the United States.
In some ways, they are different.

Jobs Away from Home

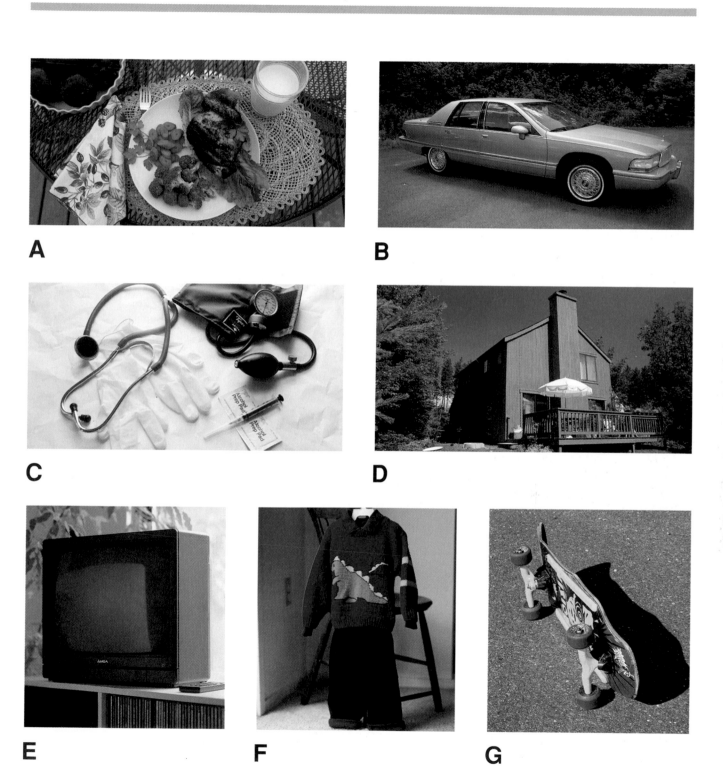

A

B

C

D

E

F

G

People work to meet needs and wants.

27

Jobs at Home

Some jobs can be done at home.

Having Fun in a Family

Families do many things for fun.

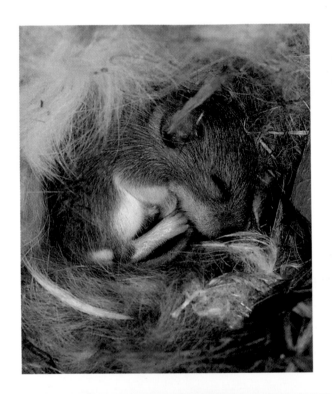

HOMES

People Build Homes

A

B

C

D

E

F

G

H

People use many different materials to build homes.

Homes of Long Ago

Long ago, people made many different
kinds of homes.

They used materials they could find nearby.

Homes Far Away

A

B

C

D

Some homes are good for warm climates.
Some homes are good for cold climates.
Some homes are good for climates where it is
sometimes warm and sometimes cold.

When Winter Changes to Spring

It is spring all over the United States.
It is warm in some places
and cold in other places.
It is sunny in some places
and rainy in other places.

Using a Room Map

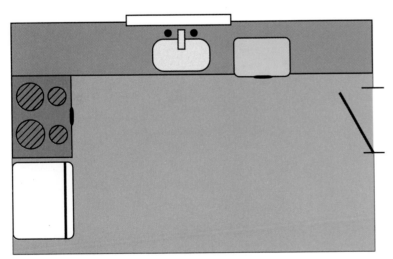

The picture shows what a kitchen looks like from overhead.
What does the map show?

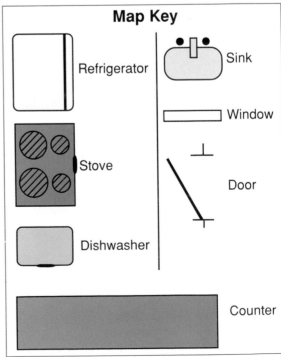

Map Key

Refrigerator

Sink

Window

Stove

Door

Dishwasher

Counter

Using a Home Map

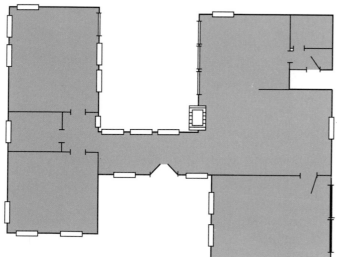

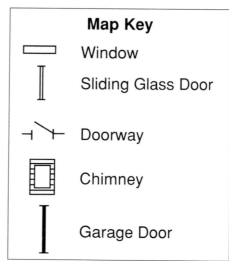

Map Key

☐ Window

⌶ Sliding Glass Door

⊣ ⊢ Doorway

▭ Chimney

| Garage Door

The picture shows a house.
What does the map show?

NEIGHBORHOODS

Where I Live

Which picture shows a city?
Which picture shows a town?
Do you live in a city or a town?

A Farm Home and Neighborhood

This picture shows a farm.
Do you live on a farm?

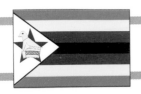

Farm Life Far Away

In some ways, farm life in Zimbabwe is
like farm life in the United States.
In some ways, it is different.

A City Home and Neighborhood

Many people live in cities.
How is life in a city like life
in a town or on a farm?
How is it different?

City Life Long Ago

People lived in cities long ago.
How has city life changed from
the way it used to be?

City Life Far Away

In some ways, city life in Zimbabwe is
like city life in the United States.
In some ways, it is different.

When Spring Changes to Summer

Everglades National Park, Florida

Grand Canyon National Park, Arizona

Haleakala National Park, Hawaii

Voyageurs National Park, Minnesota

PHOTO CREDITS